Gerald Dawe was born in Belfast in 1952 and educated at Orangefield Boys' School, University of Ulster and National University of Ireland, Galway. He has published seven collections of poetry, including *Sunday School* (1991), *The Morning Train* (1999), *Lake Geneva* (2003) and *Points West* (2008). He has also published *The Proper Word: Collected Criticism* and *My Mother-City* (2007). A fellow of Trinity College, Dublin, Gerald Dawe lives in Dun Laoghaire, County Dublin.

By the same author

SHELTERING PLACES

Poems from the seventies
Revisited

SHELTERING PLACES

Gerald Dawe

GERALD DAWE

with a preface by
Thomas Kilroy

for John, Patsy
with much love
from gerry
Creel Restaurant,
westport, Co. Mayo
10 October 2008

THE STARLING PRESS
2008

Published by
The Starling Press
112 Deramore Avenue
Belfast BT7 3ES

ISBN: 978 0 9559468 0 6
Author: Dawe, Gerald
Title: Sheltering Places
2008

Printed by
J.H. Haynes, Sparkford, Somerset

for Bob and Norma Richardson

History

Nourishes these broken flutings,
These crowns of acanthus
And the crow settles her garments.
                    —Sylvia Plath, 'The Manor Garden'

Contents

For we come as old-style wanderers
On foot, self-conscious and eager—
To watch a cleft-footed mule hike
A load up some crazy laneway

And wait until dawn before going back,
When the day will be bright
And no furtive checkpoints appear
Out of nowhere overnight.

We go back to where people die
For an Ireland of eighteen hundred
And something, and have by noon
Settled again in the city's dereliction.

When *Sheltering Places* (1978) first appeared what was
remarkable in a first collection was the degree of confidence

and settlement in the tone of voice. Here was a distinctly Northern voice but without any of the showy effects or tribal pieties that had marked so much of Irish poetry in the second half of the twentieth century. The strength of presence, on the other hand, is to be found in the moral tone of the poems, their discriminations, their weighing of meaning in closely observed surroundings. These poems are a testament to a Protestant heritage, to the decency and quiet dignity of a people often neglected behind the bluster and loud-mouthing of politicians.

But the poems in this early collection are already moving backward and forward across that benighted border with a freedom that is shaped by an acute political intelligence, one that is well above simple-minded slogans. One of the striking things about reading *Points West* (2008), Dawe's new collection of poems, is the extent of his journeying away from but always back to Belfast. This recent work is a poetry of Europe and America as well as a poetry of Ireland.

There is no escapism in this. Gerald Dawe had already met the streets of violence head-on in his early work in poems like 'Border-crossing' and 'Count.' There is a personal opening-up to suffering here, particularly in the second of these poems. The act of counting becomes a way of registering the numbed reaction to the news of the brutal killing of a friend.

But there is also another kind of response to brutality in Dawe, in the equanimity, the perspective with which he views the process of history in action, as in 'Border-crossing.'

> We go back to where people die
> For an Ireland of eighteen hundred
> And something, and have by noon
> Settled again in the city's dereliction.

Everything hinges on that 'something,' the vagueness that finally settles on all human aspirations with the passage of time however hot they may have been in the first place. This is exactly the kind of discrimination that Dawe brings to bear not only upon public issues but on the secret motions of feeling and behaviour as well.

'Border-crossing' should be acknowledged as one kind of response by Dawe to the North's political turmoil. 'Count' seems to me to be one of the finer short elegies to have emerged out of that awful period of recent Irish history.

The other poems that remain with me from *Sheltering Places* are, like the title one, highly characteristic of this poet's domestic interiors, in praise of the *domus*, sometimes under siege from outside forces, man-made or natural. This domesticity is the starting point of the inner journeying of the poet, as opposed to the geographical, and it makes up the bulk of the poetry, a search for fidelities that he needs in order to face the assaults of the everyday.

There is one other kind of poem from this early volume to which I'd like to refer. This is the kind of poem that evokes Dawe's own Belfast extended family. He was to go on and write movingly about this background, over the years, in verse and prose such as *My Mother-City* (2007). I have found this writing fascinating.

In doing so he has vividly realized not only the map of his own personal growth but a whole segment of Northern social history unknown to many of us in the South of Ireland and beyond these shores. The poem 'From Two' is one such example, a lovely portrait of a sickly child (a 'slow starter,' and with a 'chest like a concertina') surrounded by the mysteries of adulthood and a mother's love. A Grandma and other spectres stand off, mere 'Photographs in a brown suitcase.'

This personal world (and his separation from it) underlies much of Gerald Dawe's poetry, an anchorage that never quite completely holds him in place but continues to draw him back nevertheless. It informs his own development as a person, his meditations upon Northern Ireland and his critical if humane observations on life in the Republic. It would be wrong, however, to suggest that his writing about the South is merely social or political. There is, for example, a whole seam of lyrics that beautifully renders the sights and sounds, the textures of life, in a wet West of Ireland. Nor would it be right to limit the effects of this poetry to social record. There is always that probing, moral mind that raises the issue above the local to 'the imperfect state of man'.

Thomas Kilroy
Kilmaine
County Mayo

SHELTERING PLACES

At Inishowen

The last time
 Like liberty
Full of power
 Stern destiny
The sea in cove
 Great Atlantic
And Inishowen
 Glowing with
Tilly-lamp tales
 Of men gone off
From Foyle
 Standing there
At the mouth
 Of the siege
My own city
 Searchlights
Rocks and mists
 To pin me down
No shadows
 No-chance play
At the strife
 That kept scholars
And students up
 To their necks
In Latin work
 The freezing wind
Blasts from land
 To the rock face
High over Magilligan.
 We know our place.

Bloody Foreland

No man could stand here long
Where the Atlantic rises up
And the Foreland hangs across ...
The huge stones rumble.

There is only one life here
Watching and knowing
Like the gull,
Hovering and screaming,
To plunge
And glide
And cry again
That shrill pitch
Like widows keening.

Once, in the city,
Sauntered into
The wrong kitchen house,
Them all in black
In a dark parlour
Baying to the moon
An archaic death ...
The stones applaud.

You cannot turn
And walk and speak
Of our past
As something natural.

Morning Shores

The ways out have changed
But not the facts of going.
Before, they gathered along
Morning shores and waited
For the heavy ships to
Weigh in.
    Then it was
A necessity rooted
In stinking land, hope-
Less crops that weaned
A new generation to hope:
Memories tarred with despair.
You couldn't live there.
And others sailed out
Desperate for revenge,
Sat in civilised houses
And wrote till famous,
Their plight fed
On images of the dead.
They weren't among the dying.

On the Road

On the road he'd been,
Hitched across the waste of Ireland
To see the back end of Dublin;
Came to bide his time in Sligo,
With his basketball boots,
Ex-army jacket, rocking in a chair
By the fire in a pub in Sligo.

It could have been the dumb accent,
The hamstrung words hammering across
A tinkling silence, but he turned,
Pulled up a chair, told us his life
And retracted: 'It's really heavy
Up there in the north,
Really heavy, man'.

He bent back and faced us.
There was nothing more to say.
He had made his summary,
Talked us out with stories
Of Amsterdam, Berlin, Hamburg,
The great cities shining in his mind
Like glorious revolving globes.

Border-crossing
for Joe Bradley

Underground just the managed turf
Breasted into slabs for the cornerstone
Of our ritual fire. I walk around
Knowing hardly a soul. The kids,

Their keen faces turned towards Dublin,
Think I'm French. A friend retorts
In Irish and they refrain in
A preciously broken Irish

For we come as old-style wanderers
On foot, self-conscious and eager—
To watch a cleft-footed mule hike
A load up some crazy laneway

And wait until dawn before going back,
When the day will be bright
And no furtive checkpoints appear
Out of nowhere overnight.

We go back to where people die
For an Ireland of eighteen hundred
And something, and have by noon
Settled again in the city's dereliction.

From Two

I was born between four walls.
The midwife stroked my head:
'Germanic, a clever one!'
Then the doctor came, a thin thing,
She lasted till I was twelve.

A slow starter though,
A chest like a concertina,
I was laid on couches to rest
When you sang songs
To ease me to sleep.

I can remember shouts
And on the landing a fight,
A man who talked quietly to me
Before you came again
And I was safe.

I played in corners till feeding time,
Nothing different that my hands
Couldn't touch and know.
Grandma and the rest
Were just silly sayings,

Photographs in a brown suitcase,
An old house gone.
But I can peer at my hands,
And stretch them out.
Sense is something bare and animal.

'I wasn't a child at all—'.

Sheltering Places

It's been pelting down
All night the kind
Of rain that drenches
To the bone

And a dirt storm
In the car park.
The hot wind carries
Thunder making girls

Scream and old men
Count the seconds,
Improvising distance
As you shout to

Turn the lights out,
Pull down the blinds
So that lightning can't
Get in and frazzle us up

In the curtain-dark room,
The rumbles near and
Shattering flashes
Make everything go numb.

The storm is reaching
Home territory, stretching
Over the hills down
Into our sheltering places.

It Always Happens

It always happens like this
I was told.
First a pain, then a dagger,
And then the room closes in.

I can only see a cross
And a knife—
   A candle,
   A spade.
There are women in bronze,
Painted gold, swaying and
Smiling to me.
And men in steel and iron
Looking like the moon,
And a priest sitting cross-
   Legged like a garden Buddha.

It always happens like this,
In a closed room, like a mouse
Skittering about the floor.
It always happens like this,
So I was told.

Candlelight

Sitting prim as a baby
I derive power from
Screams and carelessness.

My puppets were love's
Beck and call,
Deranging floor, roof,

The whitewashed wall.
In my adorable oblivion
I cradled the world

In circus mirrors,
And night brought its toys—
Tall bottle-men

Who bent and kissed
Curtain, pillow, door.
Our invisibilities collide.

I grow close to the shadows,
Halo of fear
In the candlelight.

Dream Burials

I

We hawked the bodies up the old burial grounds,
Pulled them by the hair of the head
For they were dead as meal sacks.
And we stood like gaolers when crosses were rammed
Into place like nails hammering down the coffins
Of our nightmare dead.

II

With the stuff hanging out of him
I took him for dead but not so, his head
Nods and shakes. *Where?* Some place old
With banging windows and shrieking owls
But no one to ask save cold windy stairs
And rusty grass. His tongue wagged,
Its tip flicked like a snake.

III

Winnowing above the rock-head
Cawing gulls.
'Poor souls lost at sea.'
All night the night
Is separated by the clear bell
Of your cry.

Bad Blood
for Padraic Fiacc

We grew out of slob lands when the ice-pack shrank.
We walk upon a river that runs underneath streets
Like a haemorrhaged vein pumping bad blood.

The city suffers its black-heart houses, wastelands
Grown from a century's worth of tenements
And men sniffing dock poison,

Skin gets livid white till words come
Like those a sick man speaks:
We've grown to live with it.

The Question

You tramped around the town
With half-baked notions
In your head of hunting down
Finality in faces and stone buildings.

Nothing stood its ground.
Name-saked streets led
To blunt and bitter expressions.
Everyone had blood on their hands.

The contract was exploited,
Half-truths about 'A People'
Who marched to the call
Of imagination, all-in-all.

It was no good.
People and image were dead.
The natal relationship
Was cracking at the seams,

Unconscious it threw up
The truth, not dreams.
Brutal smashed ideals
Like bits of glass

On the roadside.
Who bent down to ask
Why he died or her,
Any of us?

Black Cat

When it gets darker
Any room is familiar—

You see things clearer
Like a cat.

Presence is a body
Bare like breath,

The window
No one's going to jump from,

The chair
Safe as a house.

But there's always more,
Something awkward

To get used to—
The place where a kid says,

My coat's a bomb,
And a man walks
With a coffin, terrified and dumb.

Names

They call this 'Black North',
Black from the heart out.
It doesn't matter about
Particularities when mouths
Mumble the handy sayings
And day-in minds tighten.

I've been here having thought
Nowhere else was possible.
A condition of destiny or what
The old generations only fumbled
With: conceit, success, a fair
Share of decent hardship.

In this extreme, perched
On the edge of the Atlantic,
You feel to look down
And gather around the details,
Thinking to store them away,
Bundle and pack in the exile's way.

Line up and through the turn-
Stile, click the ticket
And wait till you're clear of it.
You need never recall
The other names.

Count

My only problem is your death
When the radio was stuttering
Over breakfast in this flat,
The predicted west gale welting
Around our postage stamp garden,
A fat crow crouched under the wall,

And the early morning warmth
Dazed, an impractical consciousness
Footering with cups and toast laid
In their apparent order,
When first I heard your name.
It sounded crazy, somehow or other

As incoherent as a dream:
Your name, age, place of birth,
And then the on the spot commentary
Reasoning details of why and how they
Waited in a car for you coming out
Of a huckster shop with cigarettes

And pumped six bullets: five when you
Sprawled on the street. It's hard to
Make that count. The boy that did it
Was a few years younger. Twenty years,
Six bullets, nine in the morning.
I toy like a child with these numbers.

First Love

This is the worst time to bother memory.
It plays up bad like a sickly child.

But there's no avoidance, thanks to a mind
That's bogged down and must work over
The past till it's fixed and right.

A new room for love!
We started off like dazzled honey-mooners
And ended-up ripe old bitches and bastards.

Same hour, wrong time.
Why go over it all like a girning kid
That needs the light kept on?

1974

It's all old hat now—the time
We just missed the Provo bombs in Coleraine,
Final year exams during the Workers' Strike,
And meeting up again under the huge dome
Of the Central Library in sealed-off Belfast—
We were starlings flying by the night.

Memory
for Bridget O'Toole

It is a desert of rock
The rain has finally withered
Till we are left black
Dots on a shrinking island.

We come like pilgrims
Wandering at night through
The dim landscape. A blue
Horizon lurks behind whin
Bushes and narrows to pass
The pitch-black valley.

We are at home. A place as
Man-forsaken as this must
Carry like the trees a silent
Immaculate history. Stones
Shift under the cliff's shadow.
Nearby the tide closes in,
Master of the forgotten thing.

Settlements

I

When the sea comes, morning is near.
The wind carries such memories as we are able for—

Like the withered tree shrunk in the groin
Of a bog valley, where a stone-built house has fallen

Some night into the past and the echoes
Are of fields grown centuries old and wild.

II

Driving on bog roads we pass no one.
Just the sheep gaze from scrabble fields.

Abandoned houses on the hills we climb
And leave behind without time to distinguish

One from another, are lookout posts.
The headlamps dip into emptiness.

III

The car lurches forward in the darkness.
Our world has grown accustomed

To the silence, we speak only when signposts
Define distance, expecting the map to prove dead right,

An ordinance between night
And the time of our arrival.

Supreme Fiction

I

A body is stunned by this wind.
The mind spins like a coin tossed up.
Away out in the country, you were skinned
By bad luck. Turf fires that never lit!

So this was your rage for order,
Standing like a scarecrow when mists
Swept off the broad Atlantic,
Folding you in silence, numb.

II

At the raw tree root, nestling,
The entranced neck seizes premonition.
A great wing flap and the swan
Is stretched in a feud of exultation.

III

You deal in barren landscapes
Of an ice-born Atlantic
Where the trees are all bent
And scattered birds reel.

That is your own place,
Going back as if something,
An heirloom or memory, had
Been lost or misplaced.

Watching the mountains
No one has crossed,
Whatever you came for
Does not remain.

Weir Gate
for Dorothea

Whoever sits at this gate
To the river breathes chill winds.
The rust of mangled sluices
Stains the grass.

Here I saw a dying salmon
After spawn roll like a bottle
Through the narrow water pass,
The soft cup of its mouth wide open,

Flowing slowly to the sea.
Further up the water builds
And a fearful current swirls.
The mind is a child waylaid

Down into the grey blue monotony
Of the sea, and there
A restless memory can be lost
As if forever.

Acknowledgements

Sheltering Places was first published in 1978. For this revised edition, a few titles have been changed, two poems withdrawn and another added to the original. The poems appeared in *The Anglo-Welsh Review, Atlantis, The Irish Press, Stand, St. Stephen's*, in the anthologies *Irish Poets 1924-1974* (Pan), *Soundings* (Blackstaff) and *The Wearing of the Black* (Blackstaff), and in two pamphlets published in 1976, *Blood and Moon* (Lagan) and *Heritages* (Aquila/Wayzgoose). In addition, some were broadcast on BBC Northern Ireland and on RTE. A special edition of *Sheltering Places* to accompany an exhibition by Noel Connor based around this collection and another sequence of poems, *Company*, was published in 1993.

Thanks and acknowledgement is due to David Marcus, for his priceless support and encouragement in the late 1960s and early 1970s, when these poems were first written and published.

GD
2008

Contemporary Reviews of *Sheltering Places*

'No one has captured so well the incongruity of the ordinary amid the extraordinary tensions of violence and sudden death'
—*Eire/Ireland*

'The ambivalence of tone is an accomplished one. Dawe's compact, short lines, the well-turned 'open' stanzas, the controlled, precise diction—all can shape and point a balance, suggest the contradictions inherent in the subject-matter'
—*Poetry Wales*

'An impressive first collection...effective emotional reticence and deft feel for rhythmic modulation that is alive with unexplicated meaning'
—Terry Eagleton, *Stand*

'A feeling of unpadded completeness and unforced structure'
—Alasdair MacLean, *Times Literary Supplement*

'Only Ciaran Carson and Gerald Dawe actually set the Irish world against a contemporary reality, rootless and ubiquitous'
—*London Magazine*